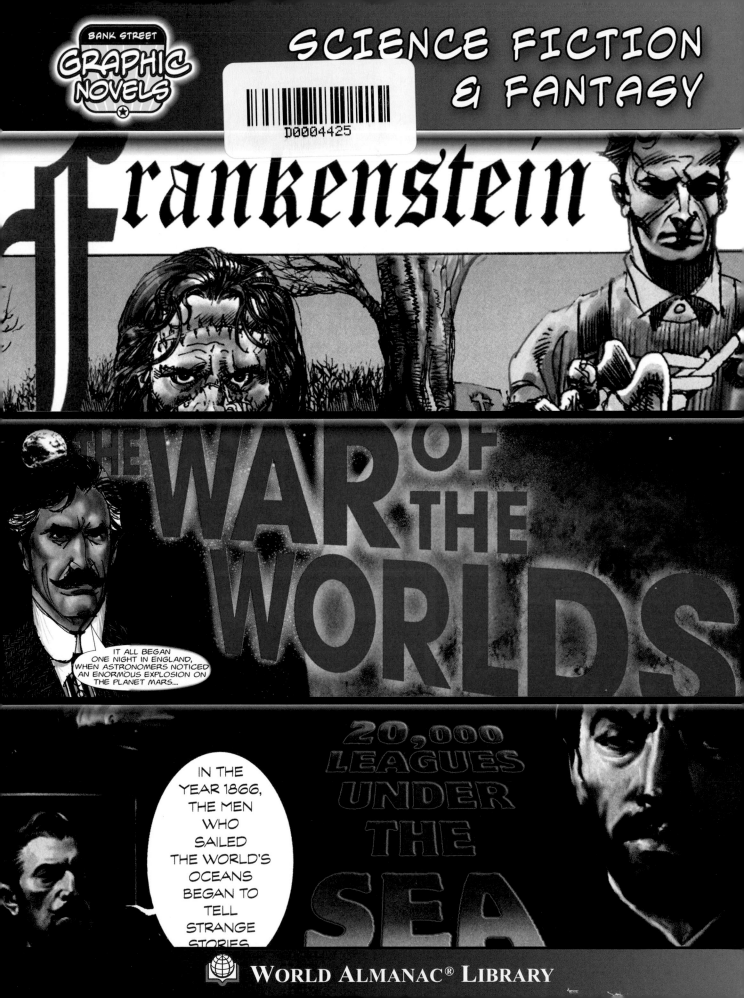

A note from the editors: These stories reflect many of the values, opinions, and standards of language that existed during the times in which the works were written. Much of the language is also a reflection of the personalities and lifestyles of the stories' narrators and characters. Readers today may strongly disagree, for example, with the ways in which members of various groups, such as women or ethnic minorities, are described or portrayed. In compiling these works, however, we felt that it was important to capture as much of the flavor and character of the original stories as we could and to use art that also captures the spirit of the lives and times of the stories and characters. Rather than delete or alter language that is intrinsically important to literature, we hope that these stories will give parents, educators, and young readers a chance to think and talk about the many ways in which people lead their lives, view the world, and express their feelings about what they have lived through.

Please visit our Web site at: www.garethstevens.com
For a free color catalog describing World Almanac® Library's
list of high-quality books and multimedia programs,
call 1-800-848-2928 (USA) or 1-800-387-3178 (Canada).
World Almanac® Library's fax: (414) 332-3567.

Library of Congress Cataloging-in-Publication Data available upon request from publisher.
Fax (414) 336-0157 for the attention of the Publishing Records Department.

ISBN-13: 978-0-8368-7929-2 (lib. bdg.)
ISBN-13: 978-0-8368-7936-0 (softcover)

This North American edition first published in 2007 by
World Almanac® Library
A Member of the WRC Media Family of Companies
330 West Olive Street, Suite 100
Milwaukee, Wisconsin 53212 USA

"Mary Shelley's Frankenstein" adapted by Seymour Reit, illustrated by Ernie Colón from *Frankenstein, or The Modern Prometheus* by Mary Shelley. Copyright © 1997 by Bank Street College of Education. Created in collaboration with *Boys' Life* magazine. First published in *Boys' Life* magazine, October 1997, by the Boy Scouts of America. Reprinted by permission of Bank Street College of Education and *Boys' Life* magazine.

"The War of the Worlds" adapted by Seymour Reit, illustrated by Ernie Colón from *The War of the Worlds* by H. G. Wells. Copyright © 1996 by Bank Street College of Education. Created in collaboration with *Boys' Life* magazine. First published in *Boys' Life* magazine, May 1996, by the Boy Scouts of America. Reprinted by permission of Bank Street College of Education and *Boys' Life* magazine.

"20,000 Leagues Under the Sea" adapted by Seymour Reit, art by Ernie Colón from *20,000 Leagues Under the Sea* by Jules Verne. Copyright © 1996 by Bank Street College of Education. Created in collaboration with *Boys' Life* magazine. First published in *Boys' Life* magazine, November 1996, by the Boy Scouts of America. Reprinted by permission of Bank Street College of Education and *Boys' Life* magazine.

This U.S. edition copyright © 2007 by World Almanac® Library.

World Almanac® Library editorial direction: Mark Sachner
World Almanac® Library editors: Monica Rausch and Tea Benduhn
World Almanac® Library art direction: Tammy West
World Almanac® Library designer: Scott Krall
World Almanac® Library production: Jessica Yanke and Robert Kraus

Printed in Canada

1 2 3 4 5 6 7 8 9 10 10 09 08 07 06

Frankenstein

PAGES 4-20

A BANK STREET CLASSIC TALE

MARY SHELLEY'S
Frankenstein

ADAPTED by SEYMOUR REIT, ILLUSTRATED by ERNIE COLON

IN 1816, SEVERAL FAMOUS YOUNG WRITERS GATHERED FOR A HOLIDAY IN A MANSION HIGH IN THE SWISS ALPS. STORMY WEATHER TRAPPED THEM INSIDE SO THEY DECIDED TO TRY TO SCARE EACH OTHER BY TELLING GHOST STORIES. EIGHTEEN-YEAR-OLD MARY SHELLEY BEGAN TO SPIN A CHILLING TALE OF SCIENCE GONE TERRIBLY WRONG....

LATER, SHE TURNED IT INTO A BOOK. AND THUS WAS BORN ONE OF THE WORLD'S SADDEST AND MOST TERRIFYING TALES.

HERE IS MARY SHELLEY'S STORY OF FRANKENSTEIN! READ ON...IF YOU DARE!

I SOON BECAME DEEPLY INTERESTED IN THE MYSTERIES OF CHEMISTRY.

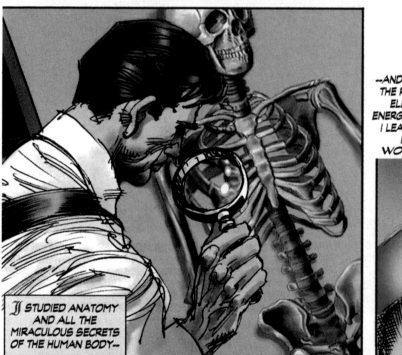

I STUDIED ANATOMY AND ALL THE MIRACULOUS SECRETS OF THE HUMAN BODY--

--AND I EXPLORED THE POWERS OF ELECTRICAL ENERGY. THE MORE I LEARNED, THE MORE I WONDERED--

CR-RACKLE!

--WAS IT POSSIBLE TO USE THE POWERS OF SCIENCE TO CREATE LIFE ITSELF?!?

MARY SHELLEY

MARY WOLLSTONECRAFT SHELLEY WAS BORN ON AUGUST 30, 1797, IN LONDON, ENGLAND. HER MOTHER DIED OF A FEVER JUST TEN DAYS AFTER SHE WAS BORN. MARY GREW UP IN THE CARE OF HER FATHER, WILLIAM GODWIN, WHO WAS A PHILOSOPHER, WRITER, AND POLITICAL ACTIVIST. THEIR HOME WAS ALWAYS FILLED WITH HER FATHER'S FRIENDS, WHO WERE POETS, NOVELISTS, PHILOSOPHERS, AND JOURNALISTS. MARY PUBLISHED HER FIRST POEM AT AGE TEN. AT AGE SIXTEEN, SHE RAN AWAY TO FRANCE WITH PERCY BYSSHE SHELLEY, A POET AND ONE OF HER FATHER'S WRITING FRIENDS. THEY WERE MARRIED

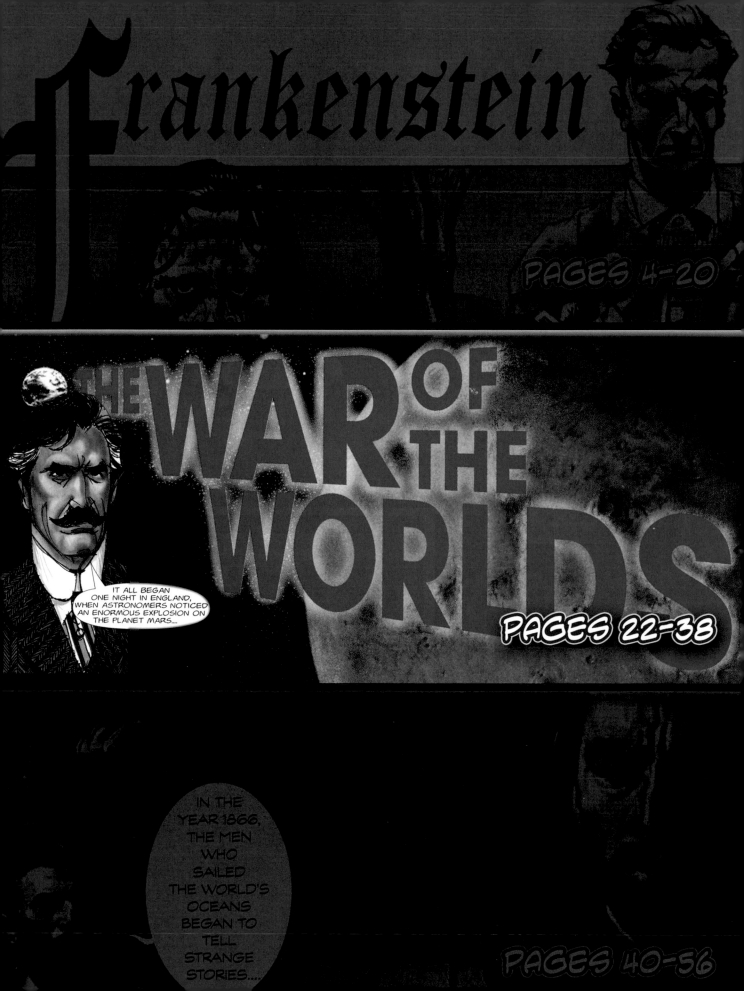

Frankenstein

PAGES 4-20

THE WAR OF THE WORLDS

PAGES 22-38

PAGES 40-56

IT ALL BEGAN ONE NIGHT IN ENGLAND, WHEN ASTRONOMERS NOTICED AN ENORMOUS EXPLOSION ON THE PLANET MARS....

IN THE YEAR 1866, THE MEN WHO SAILED THE WORLD'S OCEANS BEGAN TO TELL STRANGE STORIES....

A BANK STREET CLASSIC TALE

Adapted by Seymour Reit
Illustrated by Ernie Colon

THE WAR OF THE WORLDS

by H.G. Wells

IT ALL BEGAN ONE NIGHT IN ENGLAND, WHEN ASTRONOMERS NOTICED AN ENORMOUS EXPLOSION ON THE PLANET MARS....

THE NEXT DAY I VISITED MY FRIEND OGILVY, THE FAMOUS SCIENTIST.

ANOTHER EXPLOSION ON MARS! MOST UNUSUAL!

WHAT CAN IT BE, PROFESSOR?

I'M NOT SURE, BROWN. MAYBE VOLCANIC ACTIVITY.

COULD IT PERHAPS BE--ER--A GIGANTIC CANNON?

CANNON? CERTAINLY NOT! THERE'S NO LIFE ON MARS! WHAT A RIDICULOUS IDEA!

RIDICULOUS? READ ON, IF YOU DARE!

22

WHILE I STOOD STARING AT THE STRANGE SIGHT, OTHER PEOPLE WERE DRAWN TO THE MEADOW--INCLUDING PROFESSOR OGILVY.

GRADUALLY, THE GREAT CYLINDER BEGAN TO COOL. NOW WE COULD HEAR FAINT SOUNDS FROM INSIDE!

MY THEORY, PROFESSOR, IS THAT THIS ROCKET IS CONNECTED TO THOSE FLASHES WE SAW ON MARS!

HMMM--I'M BEGINNING TO THINK YOU'RE RIGHT!

AS WE WATCHED, THE TOP OF THE CYLINDER SLOWLY BEGAN TO TURN. IT WAS OPENING-- FROM THE INSIDE!

SLOWLY, THE TOP UNSCREWED AND FELL TO THE GROUND. I STARED IN HORROR, HARDLY DARING TO BREATHE. THEN. . .

...THE *THINGS* BEGAN TO EMERGE. IF YOU HAVE NEVER SEEN A LIVING MARTIAN, YOU CANNOT IMAGINE THE UGLINESS AND HORROR OF THOSE MONSTERS! A WOMAN GASPED AND FAINTED! I HEARD A SCREAM OF HORROR. . . THEN REALIZED IT WAS MINE!

40

WITH RELIEF AND REGRET, I LEFT MY WIFE IN THE TENDER CARE OF OUR RELATIVES.

I MUST GO BACK! I LEFT IMPORTANT PAPERS ON MY DESK.

OH, HENRY, PLEASE BE CAREFUL!

THE COUNTRYSIDE SEEMED STRANGELY QUIET. TO MY SURPRISE, I MET NO SOLDIERS. BUT WHEN I DREW NEAR THE MEADOW--

WHAT'S HAPPENING? I MUST TAKE ONE QUICK LOOK!

CAREFULLY, QUIETLY, I PEERED OVER THE RIDGE. AND I THOUGHT I HAD LOST MY MIND! STRIDING TOWARD ME WAS A FORM SO MONSTROUS, SO HIDEOUS, THAT I FROZE IN FEAR. IT WAS A HUGE METAL *THING* ON VAST TRIPOD LEGS REARING ONE HUNDRED FEET HIGH! IT WAS *A MARTIAN WAR MACHINE!*

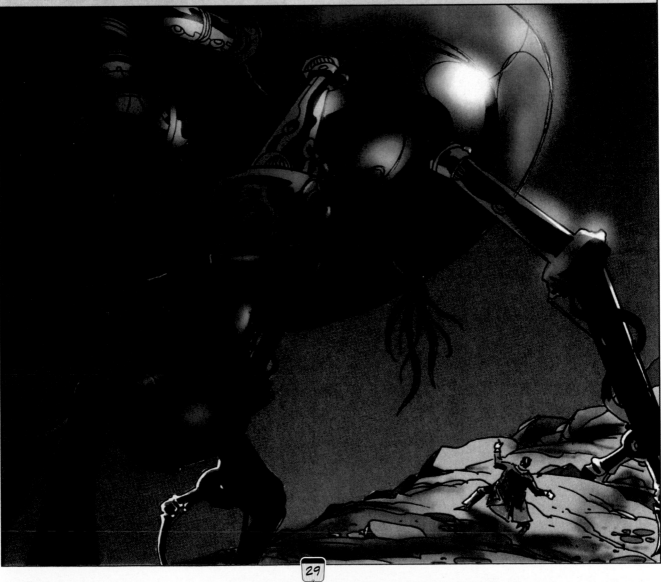

IN A PANIC, I LEAPED ON THE CART AND LASHED AT THE HORSE WITH MY WHIP.

THAT'S WHAT THEY WERE BUILDING IN THE PIT!

SUDDENLY WE HIT A LARGE ROCK! THE CART OVERTURNED, AND I WAS THROWN INTO A DITCH!

OOOH!

WATCHING FROM THE DITCH, I SAW A SECOND MACHINE APPEAR. TOGETHER, THEY RUSHED TOWARD A WAITING GUN EMPLACEMENT!

READY...AIM... *FIRE!*

THEN I SAW TWO METALLIC ARMS APPEAR. THEY FLUNG A LARGE CYLINDER TOWARD THE SOLDIERS!

THE FIRST VOLLEY WAS TOO HIGH, AND THE SHELLS PASSED HARMLESSLY OVER THEM.

FIRES BLAZED EVERYWHERE. BUT SOMEHOW OUR HOUSE WAS STILL STANDING.

WHO'S THAT?

GROAN

A SOLDIER IN A TORN UNIFORM HAD COLLAPSED ON MY DOORSTEP.

THANKS, MATE. I CAN USE SOME WATER--

COME INSIDE AND REST.

THE SOLDIER SOON REVIVED. HE WAS THE ONLY ONE LEFT ALIVE FROM HIS WHOLE COMPANY.

THEY *BEAT* US, MATE. WE FOUGHT 'EM LONG AND HARD, BUT NOBODY CAN STAND UP AGAINST THEIR HEAT RAYS AND BLACK SMOKE. *NOBODY!*

FROM AN UPSTAIRS WINDOW, WE COULD SEE THE MARTIANS COMING NEARER AND NEARER.

THERE ARE FIVE OF THEM NOW!

AYE--AND MORE TO COME!

WE SAID GOODBYE SADLY. THE SOLDIER WANTED TO FIND HIS REGIMENT. AND I WANTED TO FIND MY WIFE, AND MAKE SURE SHE WAS SAFE.

I JOINED A STEADY STREAM OF ANXIOUS REFUGEES, ALL HOPING TO REACH SAFETY.

SOON, THE MARTIANS TOOK LONDON. THEIR DEADLY RAYS AND POISONOUS SMOKE BROUGHT RUIN AND CHAOS. THEY DESTROYED EVERYTHING IN THEIR PATH!

THOSE OF US WHO SURVIVED FLED NORTH, HOPING TO ESCAPE WITH OUR LIVES.

TERRIFIED AND EXHAUSTED, I JOINED THE ENDLESS STREAM OF PEOPLE.

I CAN'T. . .GO ON. . .I MUST HIDE. . .IN. . .CELLAR--

I FOUND WATER AND FOOD IN THE CELLAR. BUT I WAS WEAK AND DAZED. I HAD TO REST. I FELT ALONE AND HOPELESS.

IT'S NO USE! THE MARTIANS ARE TOO STRONG FOR US. TO THEM, HUMAN BEINGS ARE NO MORE THAN INSECTS!

H. G. WELLS

HERBERT GEORGE WELLS WAS ONE OF THE FIRST NOVELISTS TO WRITE WHAT IS NOW CALLED SCIENCE FICTION. WELLS WAS BORN ON SEPTEMBER 21, 1866, IN KENT, ENGLAND. HIS FATHER WAS A SHOPKEEPER, AND HIS MOTHER WORKED AS A CLEANING WOMAN. WELLS LOVED TO READ AND SPENT MUCH OF HIS TIME IN THE LIBRARY OF THE HOUSE HIS MOTHER CLEANED. WHEN HE WAS TWELVE YEARS OLD, HIS FATHER SENT HIM TO WORK AS A DRAPER'S APPRENTICE. HE LATER ATTENDED COLLEGE, STUDIED SCIENCE, AND BECAME A TEACHER. WELLS WROTE HIS FIRST NOVEL, THE TIME MACHINE, IN 1895, AND QUICKLY FOLLOWED IT

A BANK STREET CLASSIC TALE

ADAPTED by SEYMOUR REIT
ART by ERNIE COLÓN

20,000 LEAGUES UNDER THE SEA

by JULES VERNE

IN THE YEAR 1866, THE MEN WHO SAILED THE WORLD'S OCEANS BEGAN TO TELL STRANGE STORIES....

WE WERE ALMOST HIT BY A GIANT WHALE, 200 FEET LONG!

IT WAS 300 FEET LONG AND VERY FAST! NO... IT WAS A HUGE MOVING ISLAND!

IT WAS A TERRIBLE SEA MONSTER, WITH AN *EERIE GLOW!*

THE MYSTERY DEEPENED. THEN, ON APRIL 13, 1867, THE LARGE OCEAN LINER *SCOTIA* WAS RAMMED BY THE MYSTERIOUS UNKNOWN FORCE.

A LEAGUE EQUALS ABOUT 3 MILES. SIXTY THOUSAND MILES IS THE DISTANCE OUR ADVENTURERS TRAVELED.

Copyright © 1996 by Bank Street College of Education. Created in collaboration with *Boys' Life* magazine.

WE WERE PRISONERS OF THIS STRANGE MAN! TRAPPED ABOARD HIS MYSTERIOUS VESSEL!

HERE IS YOUR CABIN. YOUR FRIENDS WILL HAVE ONE NEARBY.

I SEE.

THE CAPTAIN IS UP TO NO GOOD, ARONNAX. WE MUST ESCAPE.

YES, NED. BUT WE MUST WAIT FOR JUST THE RIGHT MOMENT.

AFTER MANY DAYS CONFINED TO OUR CABINS, CAPTAIN NEMO SUDDENLY APPEARED AND ESCORTED ME ON A TOUR OF THE CONTROL ROOM.

THE *NAUTILUS* CAN TRAVEL AT 30 KNOTS.* WE ARE POWERED BY ELECTRICITY WHICH WE CREATE FROM CHEMICALS IN THE OCEAN.

EVERY NOW AND THEN, OF COURSE, WE MUST RESURFACE TO REFILL OUR AIR TANKS.

*A KNOT EQUALS ONE NAUTICAL MILE PER HOUR.

OTHER THAN THAT, I HAVE NO NEED FOR THE WORLD ABOVE US. I LIVE FREE OF MANKIND'S RULES.

THEN HE LED ME INTO A HUGE ROOM AMIDSHIPS-- SO ELEGANT IT COULD HAVE BEEN IN A ROYAL PALACE!

THIS IS OUR MAIN SALON.

YOU CAN CONTINUE YOUR RESEARCH HERE, PROFESSOR.

IT WAS FILLED WITH ANTIQUES, PRICELESS PAINTINGS, THOUSANDS OF RARE BOOKS, EVEN A PIPE ORGAN!

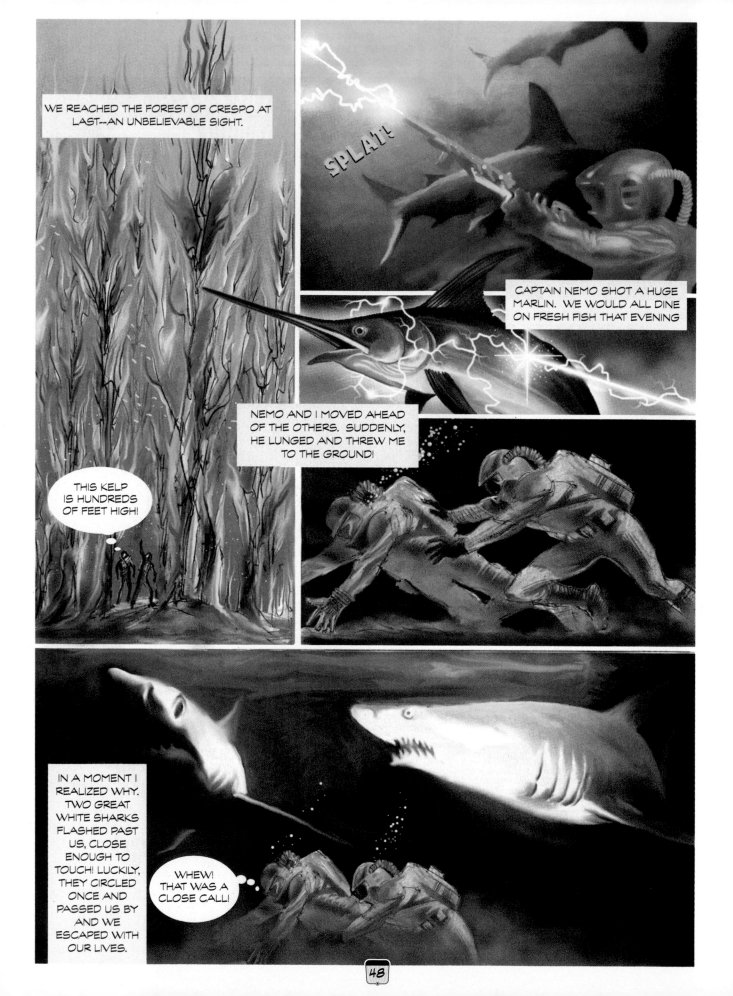

SOON, THE *NAUTILUS* HEADED INTO THE ATLANTIC, WHERE WE SAW OTHER STRANGE AND WONDROUS SIGHTS. WE SAILED THROUGH A HUGE CORAL FOREST GLOWING WITH ALL THE COLORS OF THE RAINBOW.

WE SAW LOTS OF WHALES AND A BIG, PLAYFUL SCHOOL OF DOLPHINS. THEY FOLLOWED US, FRISKING AND DIVING, EAGER TO BE FRIENDLY.

LATER, NEMO CHANGED DIRECTION, AND WE HEADED FOR THE ICY WATERS OF THE SOUTH POLE.

IT TURNED OUT TO BE A VERY SERIOUS MISTAKE.

WE CRUISED FOR MILES UNDER THE ICE SHELF. SUDDENLY, DIRECTLY ABOVE US, THERE WAS A LOUD ROAR. A HUGE ICEBERG SPLIT IN TWO!

CR-R-RA-CK!

THE BATTLE

WE BARELY HAD A CHANCE TO FILL OUR AIR TANKS AND DIVE AGAIN WHEN A SWARM OF GIANT SQUIDS ATTACKED THE NAUTILUS. THEY WERE ENORMOUS!

I DON'T THINK THEY CAN DAMAGE OUR IRON HULL, CONSEIL.

CAPTAIN, WHY DID OUR ENGINE STOP?

ONE OF THOSE BEASTS WOUND ITSELF AROUND OUR PROPELLER! WE HAVE TO SURFACE!

ON THE SURFACE, THE SEA BEASTS SWARMED OVER US! WE STOOD ON OUR SMALL DECK, FIGHTING THEM OFF WITH HARPOONS AND AXES. IT WAS A FIERCE BATTLE!

ONE POOR CREWMAN GREW CARELESS. A HUGE TENTACLE SNAKED AROUND HIS NECK.

AAAARRGHH!!

AND, IN AN INSTANT, BEFORE WE COULD RUSH TO HIS AID...

HE-E-ELP!

...THE BEAST DRAGGED HIM TO THE BOTTOM!

JULES VERNE

JULES GABRIEL VERNE WAS A PIONEER IN SCIENCE FICTION WRITING AND WROTE ABOUT TRAVELING IN SHIPS UNDERWATER AND INTO SPACE LONG BEFORE EITHER TYPE OF TRAVEL WAS POSSIBLE. VERNE WAS BORN ON FEBRUARY 8, 1828, IN NANTES, FRANCE. NANTES WAS A PORT CITY, AND VERNE LOVED THE SEA AS A BOY. HIS FATHER WAS A LAWYER, AND HE SENT VERNE TO PARIS TO STUDY LAW. WHILE IN PARIS, VERNE BECAME INTERESTED IN THE THEATER AND BEGAN WRITING PLAYS. HIS FATHER, HOWEVER, WAS NOT HAPPY THAT VERNE GAVE UP HIS LAW STUDIES, AND HE STOPPED SENDING VERNE MONEY. VERNE WAS FORCED TO WORK AS A STOCKBROKER, BUT HE STILL CONTINUED TO WRITE SHORT STORIES AND PLAYS. HE SPENT MUCH TIME IN THE LIBRARY, STUDYING GEOLOGY, ASTRONOMY, AND OTHER SCIENCES TO HELP HIS WRITING. IN 1863, HE PUBLISHED **FIVE WEEKS IN A BALLOON,**